EASY SOLOS FOR SAXOPHONE
KENNY G

T0053079

ISBN 978-0-7935-3905-5

HAL•LEONARD
CORPORATION
7777 W. BLUEMOUND RD. P.O. BOX 13819 MILWAUKEE, WI 53213

Forever In Love

By Kenny G

Slow Rock (♩ = 92)

3

Going Home

By Kenny G and Walter Afanasieff

Slow Rock (♩ = 80)

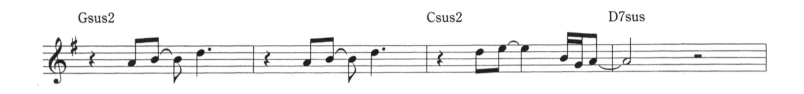

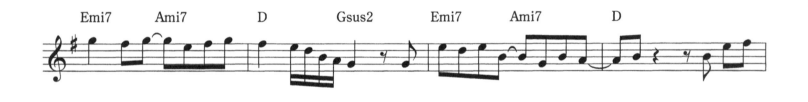

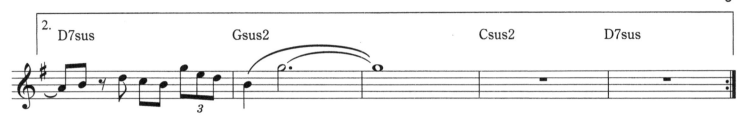

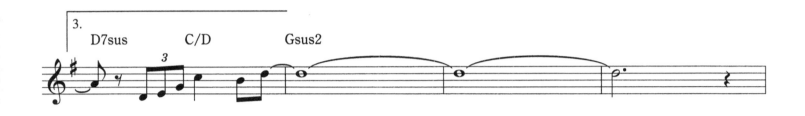

Home

By Kenny G

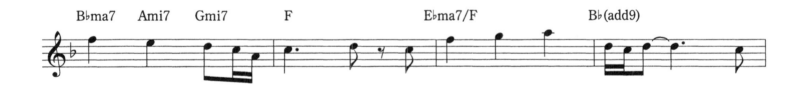

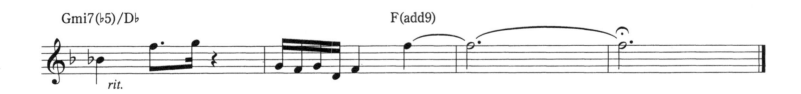

Esther

By Kenny G

I've Been Missing You

By Kenny G and Kashif

Midnight Motion

By Kenny G

Sade

By Kenny G

Silhouette

By Kenny G

Songbird

By Kenny G

Slow Rock (♩ = 72)

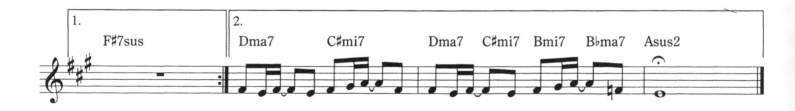

Tribeca

By Kenny G, Kashif and Wayne Brathwaite

The Wedding Song

By Kenny G and Walter Afanasieff